Original title:
Snowlight Whispers

Author: Linda Leevike
ISBN HARDBACK: 978-9916-79-591-0
ISBN PAPERBACK: 978-9916-79-592-7
ISBN EBOOK: 978-9916-79-593-4

Illumined Silence

In quiet halls where shadows play,
Soft echoes dance, they drift away.
The stillness breathes, a sacred space,
In whispers found, divine embrace.

Beneath the moon’s soft silvery thread,
The heart awakens, fears all shed.
A silence deep, like velvet night,
It cradles dreams in gentle light.

A Tapestry of Light

Threads of gold weave through the dawn,
A canvas bright, where hopes are drawn.
Each hue a story, each gleam a tale,
In every texture, the dreams set sail.

From crimson rays to azure skies,
A symphony where spirit flies.
In woven moments, colors blend,
Creating charm that will not end.

Secrets of the Frost

Beneath the veil of winter’s chill,
Lies the quiet, the air is still.
Frosted whispers on windowpanes,
Nature's secrets where silence reigns.

Each crystal shard, a fleeting dream,
Reflecting light with a silver gleam.
In icy breath, a truth concealed,
A world reborn, gently revealed.

Soft Glows and Whispers

In corners dim, where shadows lie,
Soft glows emerge like stars on high.
They flicker gently, beckon near,
In whispered tones, the heart can hear.

The night unfolds, a tender sigh,
With every pulse, the moments fly.
In soft embrace of muted light,
We find our peace in velvet night.

Mystical Icescape

In the hush of twilight's glow,
Where whispers of the cold winds flow,
The world transforms, a crystal dream,
With every breath, the shadows gleam.

Frozen lakes in silent grace,
Mirrors of the starry space,
A tapestry of white and blue,
The heart of winter's magic, true.

Glistening flurries dance and spin,
Each flake a story, where to begin?
Underneath the silver skies,
Nature's beauty softly lies.

Frosted branches, lace adorned,
A wonderland where dreams are born,
With every step, the wonders call,
Unified within the snow's soft thrall.

In this realm where time stands still,
Magic lingers, haunts the chill,
Embrace the peace, let worries fade,
In the heart of this icy glade.

Echoes of the Winter Moon

Beneath the moon's soft, silver light,
Echoes whisper through the night,
A world wrapped in a blanket white,
Embracing all, in still delight.

Shadows dance upon the snow,
Where ancient secrets come to show,
The pulse of winter, wild and free,
In every flake, a mystery.

The stars reflect in frosty eyes,
Unlocking dreams that softly rise,
Each breath a cloud, a fleeting sigh,
Painting stories in the sky.

Branches creak in gentle sway,
As the night slips fast away,
Wrapped in warmth, we hold the night,
Awash in winter’s purest light.

When dawn breaks through the icy dome,
We find ourselves, we find a home,
In echoes of the winter's tune,
Beneath the gaze of the rising moon.

Dance of Glimmering Frost

On a canvas painted white,
Frosty jewels shimmer bright,
With every gust, the magic swirls,
In a dance of frozen pearls.

Glimmers spark on fields of dreams,
As sunlight kisses winter's seams,
A ballet soft, in silent grace,
Each moment, a fleeting trace.

Chill winds sing a gentle song,
Where ice and beauty both belong,
Underneath the sapphire skies,
Nature holds her sweet surprise.

In the stillness, whispers rise,
Of ancient tales and starry skies,
With every step upon the frost,
We find the warmth of what we've lost.

So gather close, the night extends,
Within this magic, joy transcends,
As we twirl in winter's breath,
Our hearts entwined, defying death.

Reflection of Cold Light

In the stillness, shadows play,
As the fading light slips away.
Cold whispers of the night arise,
Mirroring dreams beneath the skies.

Silent waters, glassy and clear,
Echo the thoughts that linger near.
Stars awaken in the deep blue,
Casting whispers, secrets anew.

Frost touches the surface bare,
Chasing warmth from here to there.
Reflected glimmers dance and sway,
While the moon keeps watch till day.

Every gleam a story untold,
Framed by wonders, quiet and bold.
In the twilight, we find our peace,
As the heart learns to release.

Within the chill, truth unfolds,
In the depths what warmth beholds.
Guided softly by the light,
Embracing love within the night.

Muffled Footsteps in the Drift

Snowflakes fall like whispers soft,
Blanketing the ground aloft.
Each step taken, muted, shy,
In a world where echoes lie.

Frozen breath mingles with air,
Muffled sounds of life laid bare.
Footprints trace a tale untold,
In the silence, life's folds hold.

Amid the trees, shadows loom,
Guarding secrets in their gloom.
Frosted branches sway and bend,
To the rhythm winter sends.

Over hills, the silence reigns,
In the drifts, all but remains.
Nature's hush, a gentle balm,
Wrapping cold in silent calm.

Muffled heartbeats, quiet trust,
In this moment, dreams adjust.
Walking softly, time stands still,
In the drift, we find our will.

Frosted Feathers of Dawn

Morning breaks with gentle light,
Feathers frost the world in white.
Softly painted by the freeze,
Nature stirs with graceful ease.

Birdsong strums the early air,
Chasing shadows, laying bare.
Dewdrops glisten, diamonds gleam,
Waking dreams from winter's dream.

Trees adorned in icy lace,
Each branch holding nature's grace.
Winds whisper through the open sky,
As the day begins to sigh.

Frosted beauty, fleeting, bright,
In the dawn, a sacred rite.
As the sun begins to rise,
Hope emerges, clear and wise.

In the chill, warmth finds its way,
Greeting promises of the day.
Frosted feathers drift away,
In the light, we find our play.

Iridescent Chill

Underneath the azure veil,
Cold wraps round like a soft whale.
Colors shift in frosted air,
Nature's canvas, vibrant, rare.

Iridescent hues unfold,
Painting landscapes, crisp and bold.
Each breath a cloud in chilly haze,
Marking time in frozen ways.

Frosty grass beneath our feet,
Sparkles whisper, soft and sweet.
Every heartbeat, every glance,
Captures life in frosted dance.

In the stillness, spirits fly,
Chasing light through endless sky.
With each moment, cold ignites,
A symphony of winter nights.

Capture now the fleeting spark,
In the chill, embrace the dark.
Iridescent dreams take flight,
In the wonder of the night.

A Canvas of Stillness

The snowflakes fall, a soft embrace,
Blanketing the world's quiet face.
In silent woods, the shadows play,
While whispers of the night hold sway.

The trees stand tall, dressed in white,
Guardians of the stillness so bright.
Each breath a cloud, each step a hush,
In nature's art, we find the rush.

Footprints track a path of light,
Leading onward into the night.
As stars above begin to gleam,
We drift into a winter dream.

A canvas pure, untouched, serene,
Each moment feels like a scene.
In this stillness, hearts collide,
Finding peace where dreams reside.

Echoes in the Chill

The echo of the winter's breath,
Sings softly of forgotten depth.
Beneath the frost, the whispers flow,
Tales of warmth the cold can’t know.

Branches creak in the evening glow,
A symphony of ice and snow.
The moon hangs low, a silver disk,
Bathed in shadows, tender, brisk.

Frozen lakes hold secrets tight,
Mirroring the stars of night.
In swirling winds, a ghostly sigh,
Calls us out to dance and fly.

Each pulse of chill, a timeless call,
In nature’s realm, we are so small.
Yet in the stillness, we take flight,
Echoes vibrant in the night.

The Winter's Tender Caress

A tender touch upon my cheek,
The winter's breath, both bold and meek.
With every flake that falls anew,
The world transforms in a silvery hue.

The frost adorns each windowpane,
Crafting beauty from the rain.
In silence deep, the earth lays bare,
Her frozen heart, a soft affair.

As shadows stretch across the glade,
The day concedes to twilight's shade.
Stars emerge, each flicker bright,
Guiding dreams into the night.

Embraced by chill, we find our peace,
In the tender, cold release.
A moment paused, a breath of grace,
Winter's love, an endless space.

Frozen Glimmers of Hope

Amidst the frost, a spark appears,
A glimmer bright, despite the years.
In icy realms, a promise glows,
Of springtime warmth that gently flows.

Beneath the snow, the roots still breathe,
Nurturing life within the wreath.
Each crystal formed, a tale to tell,
Of hope that rises, like a bell.

In shadows long, the light will find,
The hidden strength within the kind.
Frozen whispers speak of grace,
A deeper truth we must embrace.

As winter wanes, the heart beats loud,
Emerging from the icy shroud.
With every thaw, the world will cope,
In frozen glimmers, we find hope.

Echoes of Crystal Dreams

In a world where stars collide,
Whispers of hopes, dreams abide.
Each glimmer paints the night sky,
Echoes of wishes that float high.

Through the mist, a voice calls clear,
Woven threads of love draw near.
Glimpses of beauty break the flow,
In the heart where rivers glow.

Gentle hands of fate entwined,
In shadows, memories defined.
Dancing lights upon the stream,
Cradled softly in a dream.

Beneath the silence, voices hum,
A melody where souls become.
In every breath, a story weaves,
Echoes linger, never leaves.

Time stands still, a fleeting glance,
Caught in the rhythm of the dance.
In the stillness, hearts unite,
Echoes dance in the moonlight.

Shattered Silence of Ice

Crimson cracks in icy glass,
Whispers of time slowly pass.
In the stillness, shadows creep,
Secrets held that silence keeps.

Frozen echoes softly sigh,
Beneath the frost where dreams lie.
Sharp breaths cut through the calm night,
Shattered truths take fragile flight.

Lonely winds begin to wail,
Chilling tales of love's frail trail.
In the void, a heartbeat lost,
Ice-bound thoughts at such a cost.

Muffled cries in bitter frost,
In the silence, warmth is lost.
Yet beneath the cold veneer,
Lurking hope starts to draw near.

Every flake, a tale to tell,
In frozen realms where shadows dwell.
Though the silence might hold sway,
Life will find its thawing way.

Whispers in the Frost

Beneath the moonlight, whispers sigh,
Secrets drift where cold winds lie.
Frosted branches, a lace design,
Nature's breath, a soft divine.

Silent nights, the world at rest,
In the stillness, dreams are pressed.
Echoes dance on winter's breath,
Whispers linger, defying death.

In the hush, the heartbeats tremble,
A soft light where shadows assemble.
Golden glows in crisp night air,
Snowflakes fall, a tender prayer.

Crystals form on windows grey,
Magic woven in ballet.
Through the frost, the spirits weave,
Whispers tell what we believe.

Each soft glimmer holds a plea,
Nature's sigh, a symphony.
In the night, where silence hides,
Whispers echo, hope abides.

Moonlit Silhouettes

Underneath the moon's embrace,
Shadows dance in silent grace.
Figures waltz in silver light,
Drawing dreams from depths of night.

Trees stand tall, their shapes unclear,
Whispers float on the still air.
Branches reach with ancient tales,
In the night, where longing swales.

A gentle breeze stirs the dark,
Carrying a distant lark.
Moonlit paths unfold anew,
Guiding hearts to paths they knew.

Stars align to share their fate,
Every moment celebrates.
In the quiet, echoes stir,
Life's soft breath, a gentle purr.

Through the night, a promise glows,
In silhouettes, love still flows.
Underneath the heavens bright,
Dreams take flight in soft moonlight.

Celestial Chill

The stars above gleam bright,
Whispers of the winter night.
The moon casts its silver veil,
In the stillness, dreams set sail.

Snowflakes dance with gentle grace,
They twirl, a soft lace embrace.
Each breath forms a clouded mist,
In this beauty, we exist.

The world wrapped in silent white,
A canvas kissed by frosty light.
Ancient trees stand tall and wise,
Beneath the vast, celestial skies.

Night deepens with chill's caress,
Each moment feels like a bless.
In the quiet, hearts conform,
As winter's chill begins to warm.

With every sparkle, time stands still,
In the wonder of the chill.
Nature's breath is fresh and pure,
In this silence, we're secure.

One with the Silence

Here beneath the starlit dome,
In the quiet, we find home.
Whispers fade into the night,
Wrapped in blankets, pure delight.

Frozen lakes reflect the way,
Moonlit paths where shadows play.
Every sound a gentle hush,
In this stillness, hearts can rush.

Time drifts softly, like the snow,
In this moment, let love grow.
Words unspoken fill the air,
An understanding, sweet and rare.

Together, as the world sleeps,
In the silence, magic creeps.
A lullaby of winter's grace,
We find peace in this embrace.

No need for loud and bright displays,
In the silence, love stays.
Moments melt like morning frost,
In this quiet, not a cost.

Hushed Echoes of Winter

Echoes whisper through the trees,
Carried softly on the breeze.
Footsteps crunch on powdery ground,
In this stillness, peace is found.

Shadows stretch beneath the moon,
Nature's song, a gentle tune.
Each moment wrapped in the cold,
Stories of the night unfold.

Pine trees bow beneath the weight,
Silent guardians of fate.
Frosted branches, glittered light,
Guide us softly through the night.

Clouds drift slow in starry skies,
In their arms, the silence lies.
Winter's breath, a calming sound,
In this hush, our hopes rebound.

As we pause to feel the chill,
Time, a river, gently still.
In the echoes, hearts entwine,
Winter whispers, oh so fine.

Spellbound by Ice

Glistening shards of frozen light,
Nature's beauty, pure and bright.
Icicles hang, a crystal show,
In their shimmer, magic flows.

The world enchanted, held in time,
Every branch, a work sublime.
Snow blankets ground in soft relief,
In this wonder, we find belief.

A silence deep as winter's night,
Stars above twinkle with delight.
Footprints trace a story told,
Of the warmth beneath the cold.

Oh, to be lost in this place,
Time stands still, a sweet embrace.
With every breath, we find our way,
Spellbound by ice, we choose to stay.

Every flake, a wish, a dream,
In this beauty, hearts redeem.
Together, we'll dance and glide,
In winter's spell, our hearts abide.

Hidden Light in the Chill

In the grey of winter's breath,
A glimmer stirs beneath the frost,
Whispers of warmth, though shadows creep,
A tender glow that won't be lost.

Eager rays break through the white,
Painting silence with a hue,
A promise held in frozen nights,
The dawn will rise, its brilliance true.

Branches bow, adorned in ice,
Mirrored gems in pale moonlight,
Each crystal spark, a soft embrace,
A hidden glow in winter’s plight.

Footsteps muffled, hearts awake,
Feel the pulse beneath the freeze,
For every chill, there’s warmth to stake,
In the cold, the light finds ease.

So hold the hope, let spirits soar,
When darkened skies begin to glow,
For hidden light will always shine,
In every storm, let love bestow.

Carried by the Winter Breeze

Through open fields where silence reigns,
The winter breeze begins to play,
It carries whispers, soft refrains,
Of warmer days, so far away.

Each breath of air, a chilling song,
It dances with the frosted trees,
A fleeting moment, wild and strong,
Nature's breath, a gentle tease.

Snowflakes twirl in waltzing grace,
Like secrets spun from winter's hush,
They kiss the ground with soft embrace,
While shadows blend in nature's blush.

The world stands still, yet time is fleet,
As laughter echoes through the chill,
In every gust, a heartbeat beats,
The winter breeze, a timeless thrill.

So let it wrap you, hold you tight,
This fleeting spell of frost and cheer,
For in the air, there lies a light,
That brings the warmth of love so near.

Whispers of the Frozen Heart

In the depths where ice conceals,
A heart once warm, now wrapped in frost,
Silent echoes, truth reveals,
What warmth was found, was quickly lost.

Beneath the chill, a longing stirs,
Forgotten dreams in shadows sleep,
Each snowflake holds a memory's blur,
Of love once strong, now buried deep.

Whispers dance upon the lake,
As winter winds weave tales of old,
A gentle sigh, the stillness breaks,
In crystal air, a truth unfolds.

Yet in the cold, a spark remains,
Though time has turned the heart to stone,
In each heartbeat, hope contains,
A reason still to call it home.

So linger near the frozen stream,
Listen close, the heart will speak,
Amidst the frost, live on the dream,
For love, though cold, is never weak.

The Enigma of Winter Light

In twilight hours, where shadows blend,
A mystery brews in hues so bright,
The fleeting dance of dusk will send,
A flicker deep, the winter light.

Through tangled branches, sunbeams glide,
Reflecting off the icy ground,
In every chilling breeze, a guide,
To secrets waiting to be found.

Snowflakes catch the golden rays,
Transforming darkness into glow,
As daylight fades, the heart betrays,
The charm of winter's silent show.

In this enigma, stories twist,
Ancient tales that softly gleam,
With every sigh, a chance not missed,
To grasp the warmth within the dream.

So lift your gaze, behold the night,
For in the dark, the stars ignite,
A tapestry of hope takes flight,
In winter’s hold, we find our light.

Whispers of the Frozen Woods

In the hush of winter's breath,
Branches sway, cloaked in white,
Secrets held in icy depth,
Voices weave in pale moonlight.

Footsteps crunch on frosty ground,
Shadows dance beneath the trees,
Echoes linger, soft and sound,
Whispers carried by the breeze.

Bark adorned with glistening frost,
Nature's quilt so still and bright,
Every songbird now seems lost,
Wrapped in cold, devoid of flight.

Ancient trees with wisdom share,
Stories etched in silver bark,
Fragrant notes of pine fill air,
While owls hoot their lonely arc.

As twilight paints the sky in grey,
The world holds its breath, it seems,
In stillness, night claims the day,
And dreams take wing on frozen streams.

Glacial Harmony

Whispers rise from frozen streams,
Lullabies of nature's grace,
Each note drifts on silver beams,
Echoes dance in time and space.

Mountains hum a gentle tune,
Crystals shimmer in the light,
Underneath a watchful moon,
Harmony in crisp, cold night.

Every flake, a song divine,
Softly lands on forest floor,
Nature’s rhythm, pure design,
Melodies that spirits soar.

Timeless walls of ice and stone,
Guard the secrets of the past,
Their orchestra, forever known,
In silence vast, their songs are cast.

With every breath, I hear the sway,
Of glaciers moving, slow and grand,
In unity, they softly play,
A symphony across the land.

Ethereal Luminescence

Stars emerge in velvet skies,
Glimmers spark in chilly air,
Deep within the night's disguise,
Magic whispers everywhere.

Lights that twinkle, softly gleam,
Woven in the cosmic thread,
Each a fleeting, fragile dream,
Guiding wanderers who tread.

Moonbeams dance on trembling leaves,
Casting shadows, light and dark,
Elven songs that nature weaves,
As night holds her quiet spark.

Dewdrops hold the morning's glow,
Crystals catching dawn's embrace,
In every drop, a tale to show,
Of time and space, a gentle grace.

When the world awakes anew,
And daylight chases dreams away,
Ethereal whispers bid adieu,
Yet in hearts, the magic stays.

Glint of Midnight

In the stillness, shadows play,
Midnight drapes the world in dreams,
Glints of silver, soft and grey,
Moonlight dances on the streams.

Whispers linger in the air,
Tales of old, to the stars told,
Every star a wish laid bare,
In the night, the heart turns bold.

Crickets sing their quiet song,
Nature's symphony of night,
In the dark where dreams belong,
A tapestry of silver light.

The chill of air, a gentle sway,
Caresses skin like softest silk,
With every breath, the night will stay,
Home to shadows, dreams fulfill'd.

As the dawn creeps into sight,
With warmth, it kisses twilight's face,
Yet still, I hold the glint of night,
A memory, a soft embrace.

Ethereal Glow

In the quiet night, stars align,
Whispers of dreams in the soft divine.
Moonbeams dance on leaves aglow,
Nature's canvas, a wondrous show.

Silence wraps the world in peace,
A gentle breeze brings sweet release.
Colors shimmer in twilight's sigh,
As the night unfolds, and spirits fly.

Each petal glistens with dew's embrace,
Reflecting light, a tender grace.
In shadows deep, a warmth does grow,
Carried by winds of time's flow.

Soft echoes linger in the air,
Carving moments, beyond compare.
With every heartbeat, love will flow,
Embracing night with an ethereal glow.

In this realm of night and pool,
Life unfolds, serene and cool.
With hues of twilight, hearts bestow,
The magic found in the ethereal glow.

Moonlit Frost

Beneath the moon, a silver sheet,
Nature's breath, a quiet beat.
Frosty whispers grace the ground,
In the chill, magic is found.

Branches draped in shimmering white,
Twinkling gems in the still of night.
Footsteps muffled, soft and slow,
Tracing paths in the moonlit glow.

Stars peek through the crystal haze,
Guiding dreamers in a daze.
Cold air wraps like a gentle shawl,
In the quiet, we hear the call.

Hearts entwined in the frosty air,
A moment’s pause, a longing prayer.
Whispers linger, soft and low,
In the magic of moonlit frost's flow.

Together under the starlit dome,
In this embrace, we find a home.
With every breath, we let it show,
The beauty we find in the moonlit frost.

Chilling Melodies

Winter's breath sings a chilling tune,
With every flake, a touch of rune.
Whistling winds through barren trees,
Nature croons with a subtle breeze.

Harmony of silence and snow,
Each note a shimmer, gentle flow.
Crystalline echoes drift and sway,
Guarding secrets of the day.

Frosty fingers paint the night,
In icy strokes, pure and bright.
A lullaby for hearts aglow,
As chilling melodies softly grow.

Together we dance in the serene light,
Footprints etch stories in the white.
Wrapped in warmth, we come to know,
The magic found in chilling melodies' flow.

With every note, a memory we save,
In frozen realms where souls are brave.
Let the music in our hearts bestow,
The beauty of the chilling melodies we sow.

Dances of the White Veil

Veils of white, in the moonlit air,
Softly twirling without a care.
Snowflakes float like whispers sweet,
Dancing dreams beneath our feet.

In this waltz of frost and light,
Nature sways, a wondrous sight.
With every swirl, the night unfolds,
A story of warmth that winter holds.

Chill wraps tight, yet hearts are warm,
In this dance, we find our charm.
Joyful laughter, crisp and clear,
In the magic of this time of year.

As twinkling stars join the play,
In the hush, we sway and sway.
With each breath, we come to know,
The beauty found in the white veils' flow.

Together we move in step and rhyme,
Embracing the timeless dance of time.
In this wonderland, we let it show,
The grace of life in the dances of the white veil.

Radiant Tranquility

In the stillness of dawn's embrace,
Gentle whispers float on air,
Golden hues light up the space,
Nature's canvas, calm and rare.

Birds awaken with soft song,
Breath of life in every plea,
Days like this can do no wrong,
A tranquil heart, forever free.

Breezes dance through emerald fields,
Hand in hand with shadows cast,
Joy in every moment yields,
A blissful present holds us fast.

Clouds drift lazily on high,
Cotton dreams in soft array,
Underneath the endless sky,
Peace resides in light of day.

Evening wraps the world in gold,
Radiant sun begins to rest,
In this warmth, our hearts behold,
Tranquility is nature's best.

Enigmatic Nightfall

The sun dips low, a sly retreat,
Veils of twilight softly fall,
Stars awaken, shy and sweet,
Night unveils its mystic call.

Shadows stretch with whispers deep,
Secrets linger in the dark,
Dreamers rise from weary sleep,
Searching for that hidden spark.

Moonlight dances on the lake,
Mirroring a silver glow,
In the stillness, thoughts awake,
Flowing gently, soft and slow.

Crickets serenade the night,
Filling silence with their tune,
Every shadow holds delight,
Underneath the watchful moon.

As the world begins to fade,
Mysteries in darkness bloom,
Time will weave a grand parade,
Enigmatic, we consume.

Frosty Caresses of the Moon

In the stillness of the night,
Frosty breezes kiss the earth,
Moonlight dresses all in white,
A tranquil spell, a quiet mirth.

Trees stand tall in icy grace,
Branches glimmer, crystals shine,
Winter's breath, a soft embrace,
Nature wrapped in pure design.

Footprints crunch on snowy trails,
Silent whispers fill the air,
Every star in silence hails,
Magic woven everywhere.

Winds of winter howl and sigh,
Starlit dreams float on the chill,
In the darkness, shadows lie,
While the moon glows, calm and still.

Frosty caresses weave the night,
Cradling hearts in gentle glow,
In this still, enchanting sight,
Time stands still as moments flow.

Whispers Beneath Winter's Mantle

Underneath the snow so pure,
Whispers of the earth abide,
Every flake a dream demure,
Winter's magic, deep and wide.

Fires crackle with warm cheer,
Stories told by candle's light,
In the frost, the world draws near,
Wrapped in silence, soft and bright.

Every breath a misty cloud,
Laughter dances in the air,
Friends gather, thoughts unbowed,
Shared connection, warmth to share.

Beneath the stars so glowing white,
Night encases dreams untold,
In the stillness of the night,
Winter's blanket, purest gold.

Whispers echo, hearts entwined,
In this magic, friendship grows,
Under winter's grace, we find,
Beauty in the softest throes.

Crystal Shadows

In the stillness, whispers rise,
Reflected dreams in moonlit skies.
Silent figures dance and glide,
Where the secrets softly hide.

Glinting frost on branches bare,
Casting shimmers in the air.
Every sparkle tells a tale,
Echoed gently in the vale.

Underneath the starlit dome,
Crystal shadows find their home.
Glistening traces, fleeting light,
Guide the wanderers of night.

Through the woods, a soft embrace,
Nature's magic, woven lace.
Catch the gleam, let spirits soar,
In the twilight evermore.

With each step, a tranquil sound,
Lost in beauty all around.
In this realm of soft reprieve,
Crystal shadows weave and weave.

Hushed Murmurs of the Night

Beneath the cloak of inky skies,
The world reposes, softly sighs.
Gentle breezes caress the trees,
Whispers carried on the seas.

Moonlight drapes a silver veil,
Casting shadows, rich and pale.
Stars awaken, blink in tune,
With the soft embrace of June.

Every note a story spun,
Threads of magic just begun.
Listen closely, hearts align,
In these moments, pure, divine.

Silence cradles all that's near,
Echoed dreams, the night draws near.
Hushed murmurs, secrets shared,
In this stillness, all is bared.

As night deepens, echoes flow,
Concealed wonders start to grow.
Feel the pulse of nighttime's grace,
In its arms, we find our place.

Veil of White

A blanket soft on earth's embrace,
Veils the world in purest grace.
Winter whispers through the trees,
In soft tones that chill and freeze.

Frosted patterns weave and twine,
Magic glistens, snowy fine.
Footsteps crunch in silence deep,
As nature guards her dreams in sleep.

Luminous glow, the twilight's breath,
Sings of life, yet hints of death.
In the stillness, time stands still,
Captured moments, hearts to fill.

Through the drifts, we wander slow,
In this realm of purest glow.
Veil of white, a quiet shroud,
Holds the world beneath its cloud.

Each flake dances, unique and bright,
In the canvas of the night.
Wrapped in warmth, we drift and sway,
Veil of white, our hearts will play.

Glacial Requiem

Amidst the ice, a haunting sound,
Echoes through the frozen ground.
Whispers linger, tales untold,
In the grip of winter's hold.

Blue glaciers gleam, a striking sight,
Frozen tears in solemn light.
Cracked reflections pave the way,
Glacial riddles softly sway.

Nature's breath, a slow decay,
As time weaves its silent play.
Memories trapped in icy shards,
Stories etched in frozen yards.

At dusk, the spirit wakes to roam,
Searching for its ancient home.
In the stillness, feelings swell,
Glacial requiem, a farewell.

With every shift, the world will breathe,
Carrying burdens, tales to weave.
In the silence of the night,
Glacial echoes take their flight.

Frostbound Secrets

In the hush of the midnight air,
Secrets whisper, soft and rare.
Snowflakes dance with silent grace,
Frostbound dreams in a silver lace.

Under the moon's watchful gaze,
Hidden tales in a frozen maze.
Crystal branches, stark and bare,
Guard the mysteries held with care.

Echoes linger of days gone by,
In the cold, memories lie.
Every flake a frozen sigh,
Frostbound dreams that never die.

Glistening light on a snowy crest,
Nature’s blanket, a peaceful rest.
Beneath the stars, in the stillness found,
The world hushed, the heart unbound.

With each breath, the chill sets in,
In winter's embrace, the silence begins.
Frostbound secrets softly spun,
In the quiet, we become one.

Whispers of the Winter Night

Stars twinkle in the velvet sky,
Whispers traverse the night so shy.
Gentle winds carry the sound,
As dreams in the stillness abound.

Blankets of snow cover the ground,
In the calm of night, no fear is found.
Softly falling, a quiet ballet,
Whispers of winter, come softly play.

The world draped in a silvery hue,
Secrets and stories, old yet new.
Each moment hangs as though in trance,
Beneath the stars, we find romance.

Frost-kissed branches sway with ease,
Nature's hush, a soothing breeze.
Wrapped in chill, our hearts ignite,
Embraced by whispers of the winter night.

In the stillness, our souls align,
Bound by the cold, two hearts entwined.
As snowflakes fall, the world takes flight,
Lost in the whispers of the winter night.

Ethereal Glow

In twilight's grasp, the glow unfolds,
A canvas painted with dreams untold.
Each hue a story, soft and bright,
Ethereal visions dance in the night.

Silver clouds drift across the sky,
A shroud of wonder as stars reply.
Mysteries shimmer in every beam,
In the glow, we find our dream.

Crystalline paths where shadows blend,
Momentary glimpses that never end.
Through the silence, magic glows,
In the heart of the night, serenity flows.

With every flicker, hope ignites,
Guiding lost souls through endless nights.
Ethereal whispers, a soothing song,
In the night’s embrace, we all belong.

Dance with the light, let your spirit soar,
In the ethereal glow, we are evermore.
Bathed in brilliance, forever we'll stay,
Bound by the magic that lights our way.

Shivers of Glistening Calm

Morning breaks with a gentle chill,
Nature stirs, yet all is still.
A world adorned in frosty lace,
Shivers of calm, a warming embrace.

Glistening fields, a sight so pure,
In the quiet, hearts find their cure.
As sunlight spills, cold takes flight,
A symphony of warmth, pure delight.

Trees stand tall, kissed by frost,
In their stillness, beauty embossed.
Each breath a cloud, whispering low,
Secrets held in the shimmers of snow.

With every step, the world awakes,
In the calm, the spirit shakes.
Embraced by silence, fears take flight,
Shivers of calm in morning light.

Gather the warmth, let the chill depart,
In the calmness, we mend the heart.
Glistening moments, fleeting yet grand,
In shivers of calm, together we stand.

Winter's Breath

The chill wraps tight, a heart's embrace,
As snowflakes dance in silent grace.
The world adorned in purest white,
Each breath a mist, a soft delight.

Beneath the boughs, where shadows play,
The echoes of a frozen day.
A hush descends, the wild takes rest,
In winter's hold, the earth is blessed.

The frozen brook, its tunes subdued,
In crystal coats, the trees renewed.
The night is long, the stars ignite,
A silver glow, the moon’s soft light.

With every gust, a story told,
Of ancient paths, of dreams of old.
A tapestry of flake and air,
In winter's breath, we find our prayer.

Glistening Dreams in Slumber

Beneath the quilt of starry night,
The world sleeps on, so calm, so bright.
Wrapped in dreams, so warm and deep,
As shadows blend and visions creep.

The whispers of the moon above,
Cradling hopes, like gentle love.
In every pulse, a magic thread,
Where dreams take flight, and fears are shed.

The nightingale sings soft and low,
To veils of mist, where moonbeams flow.
Each sigh a wisp, a tender tune,
As stars cascade, like grains of dune.

Awake to find the dawn anew,
With glistening dreams, our spirits grew.
In slumber's hold, we sought the light,
At daybreak's call, our hearts take flight.

A Glimmer on the Ground

In morning's light, a spark is found,
A glimmer bright upon the ground.
The dew-kissed grass, a jeweled sight,
Each droplet glints, a soft invite.

The world awakes, fresh and anew,
With golden rays, the skies turn blue.
Nature's brush paints all around,
In every hue, beauty is found.

The flowers bloom, a vibrant dance,
Each petal sways, as if by chance.
In every corner, life abounds,
With whispers sweet, the earth resounds.

The sun will rise, the shadows fade,
Each moment shines, a soft cascade.
With every breath, we’re intertwined,
In every glimmer, joy defined.

Frost-kissed Whispers

In twilight's hush, the air is still,
Where frost-kissed whispers soften chill.
The branches bow with crystal lace,
As nature dons her frozen grace.

A quiet world, a silken veil,
Where secrets float on winter's gale.
Each flake a tale, a moment's flair,
In frozen breath, our thoughts laid bare.

The nightingale rests, dreams take flight,
While stars watch over in the night.
With every sigh, a story hums,
In frosty tips, the magic comes.

As morning breaks, the sun will rise,
To melt away the darkened skies.
With every glint of light anew,
Frost-kissed whispers call us through.

Frosted Echoes of the Night

Beneath the pale moonlight's glow,
Whispers of winter softly flow.
Frosted trees in silence sigh,
Echoes linger, low and high.

Stars blink like diamonds in the dark,
While shadows dance, devoid of spark.
Each breath a mist, the world so still,
Captured moments, a heart to fill.

In twilight's grasp, the dreams take flight,
A gentle caress in the night.
Crystals glisten, painting the ground,
A serene landscape, magic found.

As dawn approaches, colors blend,
The frosted whispers slowly mend.
Yet the echoes of the night remain,
In hearts and souls, a sweet refrain.

So linger here, in soft embrace,
Where shadows twist, time loses pace.
For every echo that we trace,
Is but a memory in this place.

Luminous Serenade

A melody of light takes wing,
In twilight's arms, the stars will sing.
Luminous whispers, soft and bright,
Dancing through the velvet night.

Each note a spark, so pure, divine,
In moonlit glades, our hearts entwine.
A serenade, both sweet and rare,
Awakens dreams that float in air.

The silver strings of fate we play,
With every beat, a world's ballet.
Harmony flows, like rivers wide,
With every breath, we turn the tide.

In glowing hues, the magic swells,
A symphony where silence dwells.
Hold onto hope as shadows chase,
In this ethereal embrace.

So let the vibrant echoes soar,
In luminous serenade, explore.
The night unveils her secret art,
A timeless dance, a beating heart.

Whispering Flakes

Softly falling from the skies,
Whispering flakes as daylight dies.
Each one bears a tale untold,
Caught in silence, crisp and cold.

A gentle hush blankets the ground,
In this quiet, warm and profound.
Fractals glisten, pure and white,
As dreams awaken in the night.

Hands upturned to catch the flight,
Of delicate snowflakes, pure delight.
A fleeting kiss from nature’s hand,
Merging with all that we understand.

In frosty whispers, secrets shared,
In nature's beauty, we are bared.
Each flake a promise sent from above,
A winter's tale, a tale of love.

So pause to feel the magic fall,
In every flake, there lies a call.
Whispering moments, soft and bright,
A world aglow, pure and white.

Silvery Secrets Unveiled

Underneath the starry sky,
Silvery secrets, they don’t lie.
Whispers of night wrap us tight,
Unveiling dreams in silver light.

The moonbeams dance on tranquil waves,
A world of wonder, the heart braves.
In shadows deep where silence lingers,
Mysteries hum with gentle fingers.

Each moment captured, soft and rare,
In veils of silver, truths laid bare.
We wander deep through the night’s embrace,
Finding solace in the hidden space.

Awakening visions, bright as day,
Unraveling paths that lead the way.
With every heartbeat, secrets found,
In the stillness, hearts astound.

So here beneath the vast expanse,
Let us surrender to the chance.
For silvery secrets, when unveiled,
In the cosmic dance, we've all prevailed.

Veiled Gleams in the Cold

In the hush of winter's breath,
Soft snowflakes drift and weave,
A shimmer like a secret dance,
Beneath the pale moon's leave.

Veiled gleams on frosty trees,
Whispers of a still delight,
Nature's art in frozen pose,
Glimmers in the quiet night.

Crimson lights through curtains fall,
Casting shadows long and bright,
Each glint a story untold,
In the heart of winter's night.

Footsteps crunch on icy paths,
Echo through the silent air,
A serenade of fleeting hearts,
Wrapped in coats and tender care.

Underneath the starry veil,
Dreamers share their hopes anew,
As veiled gleams in the cold play,
In a world kissed by the dew.

Dancing Shadows on Ice

Silver blades on a frozen stage,
Twirl and glide, a fleeting scene,
Laughter echoes, hearts engage,
In this waltz of joy and sheen.

Moonlight spills on glistening ice,
Casting shadows, sharp and bright,
A playful dance, a sweet entice,
Beneath the stars, a magic night.

Gloves held tight, hands intertwine,
Circles traced in delicate art,
Every swirl, a moment divine,
Carved deeply in every heart.

Whirls of joy with every spin,
Frosty breath against the chill,
In this realm, we breathe and grin,
Time stands still, a heart to fill.

As music swells in the air,
We lose ourselves in the embrace,
Dancing shadows, light as air,
A fleeting joy we cherish, grace.

Twinkling Frosted Nights

Stars sprinkle the velvet sky,
Cold winds whisper soft and sweet,
Frosted fields where dreams can fly,
Underneath our bundled feet.

Crisp air fills our lungs with cheer,
While shadows stretch and sway,
Nature dons her silver wear,
In the gentle night's ballet.

Crystals twinkle in moonlight,
Glimmers dance on icy streams,
Magic cradles every sight,
Wrapped in soft and silvery dreams.

Hushed moments echo in the night,
Voices fade like distant stars,
A serenade of pure delight,
Beneath the gaze of silver bars.

In the quiet, hearts ignite,
Frosted nights, a canvas bright,
Painting hope in every light,
In the whispers of the night.

Muffled Whispers in White

Snow blankets the world so still,
Muffled whispers fill the air,
Softened sounds by winter's chill,
A hush that wraps us with care.

Footprints mark a journey made,
Stories etched in frosty night,
Every step a truth conveyed,
In the blanket pure and white.

Ghostly trees with branches bare,
Cloaked in white and soft as sighs,
Breathtaking beauty everywhere,
Underneath the frozen skies.

Time moves slow, a gentle pace,
Nature breathes a quiet plea,
In this peaceful, sacred space,
Muffled whispers set us free.

As dawn breaks with colors warm,
Crimson kisses icy ground,
The world awaits a new form,
In this hush, beauty is found.

Twilight's Glisten

The sun dips low, a gentle sigh,
Stars awaken in the evening sky.
Shadows dance on fading light,
Whispers cradle the coming night.

The world holds breath, a moment still,
While colors blend, the heart to fill.
Purple hues and golds entwine,
In twilight's grace, the day divine.

Beneath the branches, soft and wide,
Dreams emerge as darkness bides.
Fireflies twinkle, a fleeting spark,
They map the glow within the dark.

A lullaby of nightingales,
Each note a whisper, nature hails.
Moonlight bathes the earth in balm,
Serenades weave a soothing psalm.

In twilight's glance, all hearts align,
A tapestry of hopes divine.
As day bows out with sweet embrace,
The world finds peace in twilight's grace.

Shimmering Silence

In the quiet, secrets rest,
Silent echoes, nature's nest.
Stars stand still, the world subdued,
In shimmering silence, dreams are brewed.

A gentle breeze hugs the night,
Moonbeams weave through gentle light.
Whispers drift on a silver stream,
In solitude, we find our dream.

Beneath the canopy of stars,
Softness carries near and far.
Each heartbeat seems to softly sigh,
In the stillness, spirits fly.

Trees embrace the twilight's song,
In this silence, we belong.
Moments linger, time slows down,
In shimmering silence, we're crowned.

Only shadows break the calm,
Nature weaves a healing balm.
In the hush where hearts align,
We find the sacred, pure, divine.

Beneath the Quiet Veil

Underneath a sky of gray,
Peaceful moments slowly sway.
Hidden realms, so soft, so near,
Beneath the quiet veil, we steer.

Leaves converse in gentle tones,
Nature's whispers turn to moans.
A brook responds with calming flow,
In silence lies the strength to grow.

The dusk enfolds like a soft shroud,
Sheltering hearts beneath its crowd.
Every breath a sacred vow,
Beneath the quiet veil, here and now.

Time stands still in twilight's grasp,
Moments linger, soft and clasp.
Echoes dance upon the breeze,
Caressing secrets in the trees.

With every sigh, the world expands,
Boundless beauty, gentle hands.
In the stillness, dreams unveil,
A tender hush, beneath the veil.

Glacial Murmurs

In valleys deep where ice does flow,
Whispers linger, tales of snow.
Glacial murmurs softly rise,
Secrets hidden from our eyes.

Each crackle and sigh, a lullaby,
Nature's wisdom, asking why.
Frozen breath in the cool night air,
A serenade of time laid bare.

Mountains watch with stoic grace,
Guardians of this sacred space.
In the silence, stories blend,
Where the ice and earth commend.

Through shimmering drapes of icy light,
Dreams are woven, pure delight.
Each moment held in glacial arms,
A timeless dance, nature’s charms.

Let the echoes guide our way,
In this chill, we find our play.
For in the murmurs of the frost,
Lives a beauty never lost.

Frost-kissed Echoes

Whispers of the cold night air,
Nature's breath soft and rare.
Trees wear coats of silvery white,
Glowing softly in pale moonlight.

Footsteps crunch on frozen ground,
In the stillness, peace is found.
Each echo holds a tale untold,
A memory wrapped in winter's fold.

The stars twinkle like jewels aglow,
Casting shadows on the snow.
Time stands still in this embrace,
Frost-kissed echoes, a timeless place.

The night sky dances with a chill,
Winter's canvas, calm and still.
Every breath a cloud of mist,
In this magic, none can resist.

As dawn arrives, the light breaks through,
A world reborn in vibrant hue.
Frost-kissed echoes fade away,
But their memory forever will stay.

Glimmering Dreams in Winter

Underneath the starry sky,
Glimmers of dreams begin to fly.
Snowflakes drift like whispered hopes,
In the silence, the heart copes.

Icicles hang like crystal tears,
Reflecting all our deepest fears.
Yet within the chill, warmth remains,
In the soul where love sustains.

Candles flicker against the frost,
In this season, we count our cost.
But through the dark, light will gleam,
Guiding our hearts to dare to dream.

A blanket soft of purest white,
Covers all in restful light.
Beneath this layer, life anew,
Awakens with each drop of dew.

In glimmering dreams, we find our peace,
Harmony in winter's lease.
With each breath, a promise made,
That hope will never ever fade.

Silent Dance of Snowflakes

Softly falls the snow from skies,
Each flake a dance, a sweet surprise.
Whirling, twirling, in the air,
A silent ballet, light and rare.

Adorned like lace on every tree,
A winter's gown for all to see.
With every drift, a story spun,
An artwork crafted by the sun.

The world transforms in white attire,
Quiet whispers that never tire.
In this moment, all is still,
A sacred hush on the winter's hill.

Children laugh, their joy a song,
In this dance, we all belong.
Snowflakes fall like dreams should do,
Embracing life, both fresh and new.

And as the day turns into night,
The moon provides a silver light.
Each snowflake's flutter, a soft call,
Joyful echoes that enthrall.

Chilling Serenade

Frosty winds begin to play,
A chilling serenade at bay.
Harmonies of winter's breath,
Compose a song of life and death.

Barren branches sway and bend,
As the notes of silence send.
Echoes through the frozen trees,
Carry softly on the breeze.

Footsteps fall, a whispered tune,
Underneath the watching moon.
Every sound a fleeting sound,
In winter's grasp, calmness found.

As stars shimmer in frosty night,
The world dances in pure delight.
Nature weaves its chilling rhyme,
In this stillness, we find time.

So close your eyes, embrace the cold,
Feel the stories long untold.
For in the night, a serenade,
Calls the spirit to cascade.

Snowbound Reverie

In the hush of falling snow,
Dreams like whispers gently flow.
Blankets cover earth so white,
Softly glowing in the night.

Winds caress the silent trees,
Swaying gently with each breeze.
Footprints fade in frozen ground,
Where echoes of the past are found.

Stars above in quiet watch,
In a world that feels like a swatch.
Time moves slow, a tranquil trance,
Every snowflake, a chance to dance.

Fires crackle, warmth inside,
By the window, we abide.
Thoughts meander, lost in time,
In this moment, all's sublime.

Beneath the moon's soft, silver glow,
Nature's wonders steal the show.
In this snowbound reverie,
I find a calm, a melody.

Veils of Icicles

Glistening like jewels in flight,
Icicles hang, a wondrous sight.
They capture light in silver threads,
As winter weaves its quiet spreads.

Drip by drip, they softly fall,
Notes of winter's gentle call.
Nature's artwork, cold and clear,
Whispers secrets for us to hear.

Beneath the eaves, they sway and cling,
Frozen melodies they sing.
Shimmering in the morning sun,
A magic dance, a perfect run.

Each drop a story, frozen tears,
Memories held through frosty years.
Veils of icicles subtle, fine,
A tapestry of winter's design.

In the stillness, beauty reigns,
Through the chill, the warmth remains.
Icicles, like dreams set free,
A fragile glimpse of harmony.

Illuminated Silence

In the stillness of the night,
Stars above, a gentle light.
Shadows dance upon the ground,
In this moment, peace is found.

Moonbeams paint the world anew,
Casting tales in silver hue.
Whispers fill the velvet air,
Illuminated, hearts laid bare.

Time stands still, no need for haste,
Each breath savored, none misplaced.
In this silence, souls unite,
Bound by dreams that take their flight.

Glistening frost on branches bare,
Nature's art, beyond compare.
In the quiet, secrets thrive,
In the night, we come alive.

Illuminated, hearts entwined,
In the darkness, love defined.
As the stars begin to fade,
We embrace the night we've made.

Night’s Frosted Canvas

The night unveils a canvas bright,
Frosted edges, pure delight.
Nature's brush, a gentle hand,
Paints a world, both strange and grand.

Every tree a sculpted form,
In this chill, the heart grows warm.
Shadows play in muted tones,
Whispers echo, soft like bones.

Dreams awaken in the cold,
Stories of the brave and bold.
Underneath the starlit sky,
All our wishes seem to fly.

Patterns etched in icy lace,
Each a moment, time and space.
In the stillness, hope is found,
On this frosted, hallowed ground.

Night's embrace, a quiet sigh,
As the moon waves softly by.
In this canvas, pure and rare,
We find beauty everywhere.

Twilight's Blanket

The sun dips low, a gentle fade,
Casting shadows where dreams are made.
Colors blend in a soft embrace,
As night wraps the world in its lace.

Whispers echo through the trees,
Carried softly by the breeze.
A lullaby of the coming night,
Cradling the stars, ready to ignite.

Time slows down beneath the sky,
As day bids its warm goodbye.
In this hushed, enchanted hour,
Nature blooms with secret power.

The horizon blushes deep and red,
While light retreats to its soft bed.
A canvas spread, vast and grand,
The twilight rests upon the land.

In this moment, everything's near,
A tranquil space, crystal clear.
Each heartbeat syncs with the night's tune,
Under the watchful eye of the moon.

Illuminated Silence

In the hush of twilight’s reign,
Silence sings without a chain.
The stars above begin to gleam,
Nature holds its breath, a dream.

Echoes linger in the air,
Soft and gentle, everywhere.
Moonlight spills like silver beams,
Weaving through the world of dreams.

A moment captured, pure and bright,
In the cradle of the night.
Thoughts dissolve in tranquil streams,
Lost within the vast moonbeams.

Each shadow dances, fluid, free,
A symphony of mystery.
In every breath, a story spun,
In illuminated silence, we're one.

Time stretches thin, a fragile thread,
With every heartbeat gently fed.
Wrapped in stillness, hearts align,
In the glow of stars that brightly shine.

Luminous Paths in the Dark

Winding trails beneath the night,
Glow with whispers, soft and light.
Stars like diamonds, paths to trace,
Guiding dreams to a sacred place.

Crickets chirp in rhythmic song,
As shadows dance, where we belong.
A glow illuminates the way,
As hope ignites the close of day.

In the moon's embrace, we stroll,
The luminous paths, they console.
Every step, a promise made,
In the soft glow, fears will fade.

Through the darkness, bright and bold,
Stories of the night unfold.
With every heartbeat, we embark,
On luminous paths, lighting the dark.

A journey forged in silver light,
Where hearts are free, and souls take flight.
Together, we embrace the night,
On luminous paths, in sheer delight.

Luminescent Frost

The morning breaks with a gentle sigh,
Painting frost beneath the sky.
Each crystal sparkles, pure and bright,
A tranquil beauty, pure delight.

Whispers of winter softly creep,
As nature wraps in a frozen sleep.
A world transformed, serene and still,
As every shadow bends to will.

The air is crisp with a silvery glow,
Awakening dreams, where cold winds blow.
Every breath, a whisper, clear,
In luminescent frost, we steer.

Beneath the stars, the night unveils,
A tapestry where magic prevails.
Footsteps crunch on a crystal floor,
In the wake of frost, we explore.

A fleeting dance of light and air,
Where winter's glow is beyond compare.
In the chill of dawn, we find our way,
In luminescent frost, we'll stay.

Whisper of Ice Crystals

In silence they fall, so light,
A dance of the winter night's breath.
Crystals like stars, shining bright,
Whispering secrets of depth.

Each flake a story, a trace,
Gathered together, a blanket of white.
Nature's soft touch, a serene embrace,
Transforming the world, a pure sight.

They settle on branches with grace,
Kissing each surface, so still.
Frozen enchantments fill the space,
Chilling the air with a thrill.

Beneath their glow, the ground glistens,
A tapestry woven of magic and ice.
Each hush reminds of soft visions,
Nights adorned, so cold, yet nice.

In this quiet, time seems to pause,
The frost paints a canvas divine.
In wonder, we catch our breath, because
These whispers remind us, we shine.

Chill of the Night Air

The night wraps the world in its cloak,
A chill dances along the street.
Moonlight flickers, shadows poke,
As whispers of frost greet our feet.

Trees stand tall, their limbs bare,
Embracing the stillness, so quiet.
Breath visible, hanging in air,
In the dark, there's a touch of a riot.

Each star above, a cold spark,
Glimmers that pierce through the night.
A magic unfurls in the dark,
Wrapped in the frost’s gentle bite.

Echoes of past, in the chill,
Haunting the corners of our mind.
In the crisp thrill, we feel the thrill,
Like a story that's waiting to unwind.

With every step, the world slows,
A moment to breathe, to reflect.
In the chill, a soft magic glows,
In the night air’s silent effect.

Soft Light of Winter Morn

The dawn breaks softly, a whisper of light,
Painting the world in pastel hues.
Frosty breath gives way to bright,
As winter's chill begins to lose.

Each ray of sun, gentle and warm,
Kissing the earth with tender grace.
Awakening life in its charm,
Illuminating every trace.

Snowflakes glisten, diamonds on ground,
Morning's glow refracts, so fair.
Nature's beauty, a sight profound,
As dreams of night fade in the air.

In the hush of this early hour,
Birds begin their melodious cheer.
Life stirs softly, like a flower,
As winter morning draws near.

The soft light wraps the world anew,
Bringing warmth where cold once lay.
In this moment, breaths become few,
As we greet the dawn of day.

Ethereal Dreams in the Cold

In the embrace of winter's hush,
Dreams take flight on snowflakes' flight.
Ethereal whispers blend with the rush,
Inviting us to dance in the night.

Misty breath, a cloud of desire,
Fills the air with a tender chill.
Hearts ignite in the frosty fire,
Warmed by dreams that linger still.

Beyond the stars, a journey awaits,
In realms where the cold meets the bright.
Each flicker of hope, a door that creates,
A path through the canvas of night.

Shadows waltz beneath the moon's gaze,
Carrying tales of old and new.
In this magic, we drift and gaze,
As dreams weave a tapestry true.

So close your eyes, let the spirit unfold,
Amidst winter’s gentle embrace.
In ethereal dreams, we lose the cold,
And find our warmth in this space.

Beneath the Frosted Canopy

Whispers weave through branches bare,
Glistening jewels, the crisp night air.
Stars flicker like secrets kept,
Underneath where shadows slept.

Moonlight dances on frozen ground,
Nature's hush, a sacred sound.
In this realm of crystal light,
Dreams take flight into the night.

Blankets of white softly entwine,
Cradling hopes in frost divine.
This magic holds both calm and grace,
In winter's still and silent space.

Beneath the frost, our hearts ignite,
In the chill, we find our light.
Each breath a cloud, we exhale dreams,
Wrapped in warmth of winter's themes.

So let us linger, lost in thought,
In the beauty that winter brought.
Beneath this canopy, we see,
The wonders of eternity.

The Chill of Hidden Dreams

In the depth of winter's gaze,
Dreams lie wrapped in muted haze.
Silent wishes float and swirl,
In the frost, a hidden world.

Each breath a whisper, soft and low,
Carried by the winds that blow.
Sparks of hope in icy streams,
Beneath the chill, we chase our dreams.

Snowflakes twirl like secrets spun,
Underneath the pale sun.
Every flake a story told,
Of adventures yet to unfold.

Through the dark, our visions gleam,
In the quiet, we find our theme.
With each heartbeat, the night breathes,
Life awaits in frosted wreaths.

Hidden dreams will rise again,
In the thaw, we'll find our pen.
Write our tales in warming light,
The chill fades into the night.

Frosted Wishes

With every wish upon the air,
Frosted moments linger there.
In the stillness, voices call,
Echoes dancing, one and all.

Gentle breezes, crisp and clear,
Whisper secrets we hold dear.
Promises made in icy breath,
Woven soft with thoughts of health.

Through the haze of silver night,
Wishes shimmer, pure and bright.
Every heartbeat, soft and slow,
Guides our dreams where we must go.

Frosted wishes in every flake,
Remind us of the paths we take.
In the chill, our hopes align,
Nature's canvas, pure design.

So cast your wishes to the sky,
Let them flow, let them fly.
Frosted wonders, hear our plea,
In this moment, set us free.

Radiance in the Stillness

In the stillness of the night,
Radiance dances, soft and light.
Stars illuminate the frozen scene,
A world wrapped in silver sheen.

Crystals sparkle upon each tree,
A quiet grace, wild and free.
In the hush, we find our peace,
A moment's pause, a sweet release.

Through the dark, the whispers flow,
Tales of love, both sweet and slow.
Bound by dreams that intertwine,
In this stillness, hearts align.

Radiance glows in shadowed space,
Illuminating every trace.
In this night, with hope in sight,
We find our strength, we stand upright.

So let us bask in winter's charm,
Embrace the cold, find warmth's calm.
In the stillness, light will rise,
Radiant truth, our shared skies.

Chilling Lullabies

Whispers float in icy night,
Gentle voices, soft and light.
Snowflakes dance on frosty ground,
Sleep now comes, without a sound.

Dreams unfurl like wings of air,
In the stillness, peace we share.
Stars above, they twinkle bright,
Singing tales of frost and light.

Crimson fires, shadows play,
Holding warmth till break of day.
Close your eyes, let worries cease,
In this chill, embrace your peace.

Winter’s breath caresses skin,
A gentle sigh, soft as sin.
Cuddle deep beneath the quilt,
In this night, find dreams fulfilled.

So hush now, let night enfold,
Wrapped in stories yet untold.
Chilling lullabies will call,
Bringing dreams, the best of all.

Crystalline Glimpse

Morning light breaks through the frost,
In twilight's grasp, beauty embossed.
Glimmers dance on leaves and trees,
A crystalline world, whispers tease.

Icicles hang like nature's art,
Sparkling jewels that draw the heart.
Each breath seen like ghostly fog,
In the chill, we laugh and jog.

Footprints trace on powdery white,
Stories left of joy and flight.
Nature's canvas, clear and bright,
Captures magic in its sight.

Stars will fade but light will stay,
A crystalline glimpse of day.
Feel the pulse of winter's kiss,
In this moment, find your bliss.

Time stands still in frozen grace,
Silence sings in this sacred space.
Each breath, a note, each heart, a glance,
In sight of ice, we find our chance.

Dance of the Frozen Veil

Through the trees, the cold winds weave,
Winter's magic, hard to believe.
Twinkling frost, a blanket white,
Nature sleeps, wrapped in the night.

Beneath the stars, shadows glide,
Whispers trace where dreams abide.
In the silence, footsteps trace,
The dance of winter's sweet embrace.

Moonlight glows on fields so still,
Whispers linger, hearts they fill.
Branches bow, the winds sway low,
In this icy dance, we flow.

Veils of snow, they gently fall,
Covering the earth in thrall.
Each flake tells a story new,
Of love and light, and skies so blue.

As night unfolds its velvet shroud,
Lost in dreams, we sing aloud.
The frozen veil, a mystic sight,
In the dance, we find our light.

Dreams in an Icy Glare

In the stillness, glimmers stray,
Chasing shadows from the day.
Icy glares on windows weave,
Whispers linger, hearts believe.

Frosted dreams take wing and fly,
Underneath the vast, pale sky.
Softly calling, hidden things,
From the depths, a spirit sings.

Crisp air carries tales from far,
Promises held in every star.
Snowflakes twirl in a gentle dance,
Weaving magic, giving chance.

Firelight flickers, hearts align,
In this moment, feel divine.
Clarity in night's embrace,
In dreams, we find our rightful place.

Savor each breath, feel the chill,
In icy glare, all hearts will thrill.
As the night wraps all in care,
We discover dreams laid bare.

Echoes in a Wintry Stillness

Whispers of frost dance in the air,
Silent trees stand, stripped and bare.
Footfalls soft on the powdered ground,
Nature's breath, a hush profound.

Moonlight glimmers on the frozen lake,
Stars like diamonds softly awake.
A world wrapped in silver threads,
Winter's lullaby gently spreads.

Branches bow under icy weight,
Time stands still; it feels like fate.
Voices lost in the cold night,
Echoes linger, soft and light.

Snowflakes drift like dreams untold,
The night's embrace a tender hold.
Each moment freezes in the night,
A quiet peace, pure delight.

In the stillness, hearts align,
Nature’s heartbeat, calm and fine.
Echoes fade, yet still remain,
A timeless bond, a soft refrain.

Gleaming in the Twilight

As daylight wanes, the sky ignites,
Colors blend in soft delights.
Crimson hues and golden rays,
Glimmer faintly as sunlight plays.

Shadows stretch across the ground,
In twilight's arms, peace is found.
Whispers of winds begin to sigh,
Nature's magic, a gentle cry.

Stars peek through a velvet shroud,
The fading sun, a gentle crowd.
Evening brings its soothing grace,
Gleaming bright, a soft embrace.

Creatures stir in the dusk's embrace,
In the glow, they find their place.
Every heartbeat, every sigh,
Echoes softly, as time flutters by.

Glimmers shine on the tranquil lake,
Rippling dreams that softly wake.
A world at peace, a fleeting glance,
In twilight’s glow, we find our chance.

Soft Embrace of Winter

In winter's grasp, the world slows down,
A snowy blanket, pure and brown.
Breath of frost on winter's night,
Stars above, an endless sight.

Stillness wraps the earth so tight,
Crystalline whispers fill the night.
Each flake falls, a dance unique,
Soft embrace, the silence speaks.

Fires crackle, warmth unfolds,
Stories shared, and laughter holds.
Beneath the stars, a cozy glow,
Hearts ignite in the chilly snow.

Moonlit paths where shadows dwell,
Magic spins its frosty spell.
Winter's breath, a calming tune,
Softly drifting, beneath the moon.

So in this chill, we find our peace,
A festive spirit, love's release.
Winter's chill, a gentle kiss,
In its embrace, we find our bliss.

Secrets Beneath the White

Underneath the snowy cloak,
Whispers breathe, unspoken spoke.
Secrets held in the frozen floor,
Nature's silence, tales of yore.

A world transformed, a tranquil sight,
Blanketed in soft, pure white.
Footprints trace a story's end,
In every step, the past transcends.

Hidden gems, in snowflakes' fall,
Each one dances, answering the call.
Mysteries wrapped in gentle night,
Secrets glimmer in the moonlight.

Branches cradle the weight of time,
Every whisper, a hidden rhyme.
Beneath the white, life’s rhythms sigh,
Nature's hush where shadows lie.

In this quiet, dreams ignite,
Hearts awaken, taking flight.
Secrets, whispers, soft and deep,
In winter's arms, we softly keep.

Ethereal Frost

In the hush of dawn's first light,
Frosty whispers kiss the ground.
Each blade of grass, a crystal sight,
Nature's beauty, peace profound.

Brittle branches draped in white,
Glimmer gently in the sun.
Morning glows with pure delight,
Awakening, the day begun.

Footsteps crunch on frozen dew,
Every sound a sparkling note.
A world transformed with every hue,
In this winter's soft, warm coat.

Winds that swirl like whispered sighs,
Carrying tales from far away.
Ethereal frost, a grand disguise,
Hiding secrets of the day.

As the sun begins to rise,
The frost retreats, a fleeting ghost.
But in memory it lies,
A fleeting touch we cherish most.

Nocturnal Shimmers

Stars awaken in velvet skies,
Dancing lights, a cosmic show.
Night unfurls as daylight dies,
Nocturnal shimmers gently glow.

Moonbeams spill on tranquil streams,
Casting shadows, soft and wide.
Whispers drift like distant dreams,
In the dark, the world confides.

Silent woods, a muted hum,
Creatures stir in shadows thrown.
Lunar light, a gentle drum,
Guides the wanderer, alone.

Breeze that weaves through silver leaves,
Brings a cooling, sweet embrace.
In the night, the heart believes,
In hidden wonders, finds its place.

As dawn's light begins to creep,
Nocturnal whispers fade away.
In dreams, we slip, and softly sleep,
Embracing night, till break of day.

Whispering Pines Beneath the Stars

Among the pines, the secrets stir,
Softly rustling in the night.
Underneath the cosmic blur,
Whispered dreams take radiant flight.

Each tall tree holds stories old,
Branches reach up to the sky.
In their shade, the heart grows bold,
With the moon, the stars comply.

The scent of earth, a soothing balm,
Nature's peace, a tender touch.
Wrapped in night, I find my calm,
In the dark, I crave so much.

Owls call softly in the black,
Wisdom spoken with each note.
As the world begins to slack,
Ancient verses quietly float.

Whispers linger, hearts entwined,
In the embrace of night’s allure.
Beneath the stars, our souls aligned,
In whispered pines, forever pure.

Lunar Frosts

Crystalline flares upon the ground,
Lunar frosts that gleam and glisten.
In the silence, beauty found,
Echoes softly, stars will listen.

Each frozen breath, a silver sigh,
Painting night with icy lace.
In the stillness, dreams fly high,
Caressed by chill, a soft embrace.

Moonlit paths where shadows blend,
Guiding steps in quiet night.
With each moment, hearts transcend,
In the glimmer, worlds ignite.

Nature sleeps in frosty dreams,
Wrapped in veils of crystal sheen.
While the universe softly beams,
Lunar frosts unveil the scene.

As dawn approaches, chill will fade,
Yet memories of ice endure.
Through the light, a magic laid,
In lunar frosts, forever pure.

The Veil of Silence

In the quiet night, whispers gleam,
Stars sing softly, lost in a dream.
Moonlight dances on fragile streams,
Time holds its breath, or so it seems.

Shadows weave tales in muted grace,
Echoes of laughter, a fleeting trace.
Stillness drapes over this sacred space,
Wrapped in a veil no hand can erase.

Every heartbeat takes its stand,
Cradled in silence, hand in hand.
In this moment, life is planned,
Threads of fate by unseen strand.

Soft scents linger of earth and pine,
Nature's secrets, the stars align.
In silence, joy and sorrow entwine,
A tapestry woven, pure and divine.

Beyond the horizon, dawn will rise,
Breaking the spell where mystery lies.
Yet for tonight, sweetness defies,
Wrapped in the silence, endless skies.

Frostbitten Reveries

Beneath the frost, the world sleeps tight,
Whispers of winter, shrouded in white.
Stars shimmer cold, a haunting sight,
In frostbitten dreams, the heart takes flight.

Crystal fairies flit on frozen air,
Painting the night with a delicate flare.
Every breath visible, a breath of despair,
The chill wraps around, a tender snare.

Footsteps crunch on this icy ground,
Echoes of memories, lost yet found.
In wintry silence, hopes abound,
Love’s warmth lingers, all around.

Snowflakes twirl in a waltz so slow,
Each one unique as they dance below.
In the stillness, serenity flows,
Frostbitten dreams, a gentle glow.

Yet soon will come the thawing sun,
The icy grip of night undone.
In every ending, new beginnings spun,
Frostbitten reveries, sweetly won.

Enchanted Crystals

In the forest deep, where shadows play,
Crystals glimmer in their own ballet.
Light refracts in a magical way,
Whispers of nature, come what may.

Each gem a story, each hue a song,
Tales of the earth where they grow strong.
Under the boughs, they hum along,
Bound by the magic that's never wrong.

Dewdrops linger on emerald leaves,
Morning sun weaves through, gently weaves.
In this realm, the heart believes,
In enchanted crystals, the soul retrieves.

Find solace here in their sparkle bright,
Guiding your path through day and night.
In nature's bounty, pure delight,
Enchanted crystals, hope takes flight.

As twilight deepens, the magic wakes,
In the air, a dance that gently shakes.
Beneath the stars, the earth remakes,
Enchanted crystals, the world awakes.

Soft Light on Snow

A blanket of white, soft in the glow,
Whispers of winter, tranquil and slow.
Footprints emerge in a delicate show,
Soft light on snow, the world in tow.

Moonlit silence wraps around tight,
Shadows and dreams merge in the night.
In this beauty, hearts feel light,
Carried by calm, like a soft kite.

Flakes fall gently, each one a star,
Adorning the earth, wide and far.
In the soft light, there's peace ajar,
Nature's canvas, a glimpse of who we are.

With every breath, the cold air sparkles,
Dance of the night in gentle marvels.
Under the sky, the heart unshackles,
Finding joy where soft light rekindles.

As dawn approaches, the shades will change,
Colors awaken, dreams rearrange.
Yet in my heart, this night will remain,
Soft light on snow, forever a gain.

Glowing Fragments of Time

In the quiet dusk, shadows play,
Whispers of moments, drift away.
Stars flicker softly, memories shine,
Glowing fragments, traces of time.

Each heartbeat echoes, stories unfold,
Laughter and tears, secrets retold.
A tapestry woven, bright and divine,
Interwoven threads, love intertwine.

The past is a river, flowing so free,
Carrying dreams down to the sea.
In twilight's embrace, all souls align,
Together we dance, in sync with time.

Through the ages, we search and seek,
Cherished connections, whispers so weak.
But in the glow, there's a spark to find,
A universe crafted in heart and mind.

In each fleeting moment, joy may ignite,
Illuminating shadows, banishing night.
With hearts open wide, we'll brightly shine,
In glowing fragments, our lives combine.

The Crystal Fairy's Lament

Beneath the moonlight, tears gently flow,
A crystal fairy whispers low.
In faded gardens where dreams once spun,
She sings of laughter, now overrun.

Once kissed by sunlight, her wings bright,
Now dimmed by shadows and endless night.
With every sigh, a wish takes flight,
To heal the world, to make it right.

Through silver branches, echoes appear,
Haunting the breezes, laced with despair.
In the still of twilight, she weaves her rhyme,
A melody soft, lost in time.

Will she find solace, or fade away?
In crystal whispers, she longs to stay.
For every moment, however slight,
Holds a glimmer, a flicker of light.

Yet hope resides in the fabric of night,
As dawn approaches, ushering light.
With dreams reborn, she'll soar once more,
The crystal fairy, forever adored.

When the World Wears a White Crown

Snowflakes descend, a gentle hush,
Covering earth with a silken blush.
Trees stand tall, draped in pure white,
When the world wears a crown, a tranquil sight.

Footsteps muffled, in soft, powdery ground,
Nature's embrace, peace is found.
Children's laughter, joy's sweet sound,
When the world wears a crown, love is unbound.

Stars twinkle bright in the indigo sky,
Beneath the stillness, dreams dare to fly.
A canvas painted in delicate frost,
When the world wears a crown, nothing is lost.

Crimson and gold in the fading sun,
Evening whispers, the day is done.
In winter's embrace, the heartbeats align,
When the world wears a crown, all souls entwine.

With each flake that falls, a story is told,
Of warmth and wonder, of hearts bold.
In this quiet magic, we joyfully drown,
When the world wears a crown, we gather around.

Gentle Murmurs of Winter

Whispers of winter breeze through the night,
Softly they carry the hopes of the light.
Frost-kissed branches, glistening bright,
Gentle murmurs, nature's delight.

The world slows down, wrapped in a shroud,
As silence blankets the bustling crowd.
In the hush of the night, dreams take flight,
Gentle murmurs echo, soft and white.

Icicles hanging, like crystal dreams,
Cascading laughter in silver streams.
Underneath the stars, hearts reunite,
Gentle murmurs linger, sweet and slight.

Through the windowpanes, warm fires glow,
Stories unfold in the evening's flow.
With every whisper, love ignites,
Gentle murmurs guide the night.

As winter dances, so calm and serene,
Life slows down in a shimmering scene.
In every breath, there's magic in sight,
Gentle murmurs of winter, pure delight.

Hushed Whispers of Twilight

In the fading light, shadows blend,
Soft whispers echo, as day must end.
Stars begin to twinkle high,
A canvas painted by the sky.

Gentle breezes stir the trees,
Carrying secrets with such ease.
Moonlight dances on the ground,
In this tranquility, peace is found.

Each moment lingers, begins to sigh,
Echoes of the day slowly die.
Crickets chirp their nighttime tune,
As dreams awaken under the moon.

The world slows down, a breath is drawn,
As night unfolds, the light is gone.
Hushed whispers linger in the air,
In twilight's embrace, we softly share.

Frozen Reflections

Icy crystals cling to the ground,
In frozen stillness, beauty is found.
Nature's breath, a shimmering glow,
As winter's hand paints everything slow.

Mirror lakes hold the sky's embrace,
Reflecting dreams in a timeless place.
Snowflakes dance in the crisp air,
They twirl and spin, with grace so rare.

Whispers of winds through the trees,
An ancient song carried with ease.
Each breath exhaled, a cloud of white,
In frozen realms, we find pure light.

Footprints trace a journey unknown,
Paths of silence where we've grown.
Moments frozen in crystal hue,
Memories cast in shades of blue.

As the sun dips low on the horizon,
Golden rays through the frost are risin'.
In frozen reflections, we find our way,
Guided by light, in the depth of gray.

Tranquil Dusk

As daylight wanes, the colors blend,
Pastel skies where daylight bends.
Mountains loom, a shadowed sight,
Wrapped in soft, ethereal light.

Birds return to their cozy nests,
Nature settles, taking rest.
Whispers of the night draw near,
In tranquil dusk, all becomes clear.

The earth sighs with a quiet grace,
Embracing change, a warm embrace.
Evening's hush, a soft cocoon,
Cradled gently beneath the moon.

Stars peek out, twinkling bright,
Marking time in the deepening night.
From dusk to dawn, a sacred space,
In tranquility, we find our place.

Each heartbeat synchronized with the night,
Awakening dreams in the soft twilight.
Emotions flow as shadows play,
In tranquil dusk, we drift away.

Frosted Memories

Memories linger like frost on glass,
Whispers of moments that gently pass.
Time's gentle touch leaves its trace,
In frosted corners, we find our place.

The chill of winter wraps us tight,
Embracing shadows, holding them light.
Laughing echoes dance through the air,
In the warmth of memories we share.

Each breath we take, a story unfolds,
Of precious moments, a treasure untold.
Sprinkled like snow, they blanket the past,
In frosted memories, love will last.

Time may fade, but feelings remain,
A tapestry woven of joy and pain.
With every heartbeat, we hold them dear,
In frosted memories, always near.

So let us linger in the day’s embrace,
Amidst the chill, find a warm space.
For in our hearts, the frost may lay,
But memories shine, lighting the way.

Luminous Hush

In the stillness of night, we breathe,
Whispers of dreams weave the air.
Stars sprinkle silver, a tapestry bright,
Soft echoes linger, light as a prayer.

Moonlight kisses the world so sweet,
Shadowed forms in a gentle embrace.
Every heartbeat a rhythmic retreat,
In silence, we find our cherished space.

Time drifts softly like a feathered sigh,
Each moment suspended, held in grace.
Luminous whispers, the night floats by,
Wrapped in a hush that time can't erase.

Hearts unfurl in the tranquil glow,
As the night deepens its soft enthrall.
In this luminous hush, we both know,
Love's quiet language, the night is our call.

Together we linger beneath the starlit,
Dreams twinkling bright in the velvet sky.
In this luminous hush, we commit,
To hold forever in night's lullaby.

Frozen Reverberations

The world is wrapped in a crystalline shroud,
Silence, a blanket, heavy and still.
Echoes drift soft, like whispers of loud,
Each footstep reveals winter's will.

Frost-clad branches wear diamonds bright,
Moonlight caresses the snowy ground.
As breath hangs like clouds in the night,
Nature's still heartbeat, a ghostly sound.

Snowflakes dance in the chill's embrace,
Ghostly figures in the midnight air.
Every shimmer holds a secret place,
Frozen reverberations linger there.

Time slows down in this winter's grasp,
Moments dripping like icicles bright.
Capturing beauty in a frozen clasp,
In the whispers of the deepening night.

Together we wander through fields of white,
Tracing our steps through the shimmering glow.
In frozen reverberations, delight,
We find our warmth in the world below.

Songs of Soft Snowdrifts

Silent blankets of white softly lie,
Each curve and contour holds stories untold.
In the hush of the night, we draw nigh,
Wrapped in the magic of winter's hold.

Whispers of snowflakes in moon’s gentle light,
Creating a symphony, tender and sweet.
Nature’s soft song echoes through the night,
Melodies dance on the cold, silver sheet.

Children at play in the powdery glow,
Laughing and tumbling, hearts full of cheer.
Songs of soft snowdrifts twirl to and fro,
In a world where joy banishes fear.

Every flake glistens with fragile delight,
A moment to cherish, a gift from the sky.
In these sweet songs, the world feels just right,
Spinning and swirling, as time passes by.

So let us embrace this blanket of white,
And join in the rhythm of life’s gentle groove.
In songs of soft snowdrifts, our spirits take flight,
In winter’s warm heart, we endlessly move.

Twilight's Glistening Gaze

The sun bows low with a fiery glow,
Painting the sky in hues of embrace.
Twilight whispers secrets only we know,
In the fading light, we find our place.

Shadows stretch long across the ground,
As stars awaken, blinking awake.
In twilight's glistening gaze, we are found,
Caught in the magic that night can make.

Crickets chirp gently, the nightingale sings,
Nature’s orchestra starts its sweet play.
Every moment held in beautiful strings,
As the world transforms into shades of gray.

Beneath the vast cosmos, dreams begin,
In the serene light, our hearts intertwine.
Through twilight's veil, love's gentle spin,
Wraps us in magic, unspoken, divine.

Together we wander where shadows caress,
In twilight's glistening gaze, we unite.
With every heartbeat, we feel the caress,
Of a world in wonder, cloaked in night’s light.